by Wes Erwin

Illustrations by Kathie Kemp

Adventure Publications, Inc.

Cambridge, MN

Dedications

This book is dedicated to my sons Wyatt and Jordan and my wife Debby. You enrich my life every day.

— **WES**

For my Dad, Leon, who gazed in wonder with me at the great outdoors—and showed me how to use a camera.

— **KATHIE**

CREDITS:

Cover and book design by Jonathan Norberg

Duluth pack photo courtesy of Wes Erwin
Headlamp photo courtesy of Jonathan Norberg
Jack pine photo courtesy of Joseph O'Brien, USDA Forest Service, and licensed under the Creative Commons Attribution-Share Alike 3.0
  license, available here: http://creativecommons.org/licenses/by-sa/3.0/deed.en
Ojibwe photo courtesy of Minnesota Historical Society
Voyageur photo courtesy of Wikipedia user Jonathunder and licensed under the Creative Commons Attribution-Share Alike 3.0 license,
  available here: http://creativecommons.org/licenses/by-sa/3.0/deed.en

10 9 8 7 6 5 4 3 2 1

Text copyright 2014 Wes Erwin
Illustrations copyright 2014 Kathie Kemp
Published by Adventure Publications, Inc.
820 Cleveland Street South
Cambridge, MN 55008
1-800-678-7006
www.adventurepublications.net

ISBN: 978-1-59193-498-1

Introduction

The Boundary Waters Canoe Area Wilderness (BWCAW) is a very special place in northern Minnesota. It is an amazing wilderness area connected by lakes, rivers and portages, where people canoe, camp and experience nature. This book will introduce you to some of the sights you might see and some activities you might do when you visit this remarkable place.

Aurora Borealis

It is a beautiful and clear night in the Boundary Waters. I carefully pick my way through the dark, away from the dying campfire, and lie flat on my back on a rock overlooking the calm lake. Overhead I see shimmering red, green, yellow and white lights dancing in the northern sky. It is a brilliant laser light show put on by Mother Nature. I watch with wonder and amazement as these lights flash and glow.

The lights that sometimes appear in the northern sky are called aurora borealis or northern lights. Look for them in the northern sky on a clear night.

Blueberries

A black bear with a purple smile gobbles blueberries on a sunny southern-facing hillside. Bears love blueberries and can eat as many as 30,000 berries a day!

In the Boundary Waters people pick blueberries from low bushes in July and August. They taste much better than the blueberries from a grocery store! In addition to eating blueberries by the handful, add blueberries to pancakes, pudding or cheesecake for a delicious treat! See the back of the book for a blueberry pancake recipe. Always ask an adult before eating blueberries (or anything) in the wilderness. Some berries are poisonous and can make you sick.

Campsite

My stomach rumbles as the sun slowly sinks toward the western horizon. We have been paddling all day, and it is time to find a place to camp. We anxiously paddle toward an island campsite. It is empty! Located on a small hill, the site has a fire pit with a clear view of the lake. The towering pines provide sturdy branches where we can hang our food pack. Near the water, the site even has rocks that are a great place to fish from or jump in the water.

In the Boundary Waters, campsites come in all different sizes and types. All campsites have a metal fire grate, a space for a tent and an outdoor bathroom. A fun activity is rating campsites based on how nice they seem to you. See the back of the book for an example of a campsite rating sheet.

Duluth Pack

I tie a strong rope on my Duluth pack, throw the rope over a high branch and pull the rope until the heavy bag is far above the ground. This bag has all my group's food in it, so I must keep it safe from bears.

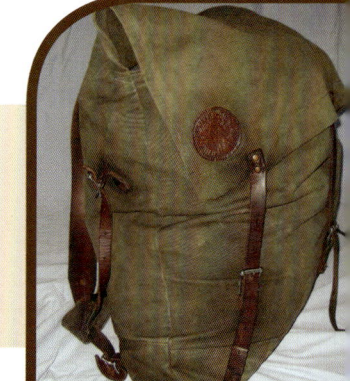

The Duluth pack is a special type of bag made out of sturdy canvas. It has a plastic liner to make it waterproof and straps to carry it on a portage trail. These types of packs were made to use in a canoe. Make a miniature Duluth pack from a piece of paper or a small piece of fabric using the pattern in the back of this book.

Eagle

An eagle with a seven-foot wingspan swoops low over the lake and dips its razor-sharp talons into the water. When it rises, it grasps a wriggling fish with its talons! The eagle flies to a large rock and eats its catch.

Eagles build huge nests high in tall trees, and they love to eat fish. You might spot an eagle perched far above the ground in a tree along a lake or river in the Boundary Waters. Use the list of birds in the back of this book to check off those you see while camping.

Fire

From our canoe we spy a wisp of smoke curling up from the fire grate at an empty campsite. We stop at the campsite. I fill my hat with lake water, pour it on the fire, stir the coals with a stick and then pour more water on it. The coals become cool to the touch, and we feel happy that we have done our part to protect this special place.

Campfires are a fun part of the camping experience, and fire is a natural part of the Boundary Waters. However, fire is dangerous and destructive if it gets out of control. Always make sure your campfire is completely out! And if you look closely, you can see signs of previous forest fires as you travel in the Boundary Waters: blackened tree trunks, scorched ground and large areas of new growth.

Glacier

A gigantic mountain of ice and packed snow scrapes across the land, pushing dirt like a huge bulldozer and scooping holes like an immense machine. The glacier picks up a big boulder, carries it for miles and eventually drops it in the middle of a meadow. This boulder is now far from the place where it originally formed.

A number of glaciers covered the area that is now the Boundary Waters Canoe Area Wilderness. They helped create the lakes, land and hills you see there. As you travel in the Boundary Waters, look for boulders, called erratics, that are found away from other rock formations. These are evidence of past glaciers.

Headlamp

My dog jumps to his feet from a deep sleep, barks in alarm, and stands growling with hair on end, facing the darkness outside the tent. I quickly turn on my headlamp and scan the campsite. Nothing has been disturbed, so I lie back down and shut off my headlamp. Unfortunately I can't shut off my imagination as easily, and images of hungry bears flash through my head. In the morning I find no sign of bears. I never find out what caused the dog to bark.

A headlamp is a flashlight that you wear on a band that fits around your head. It is a useful tool in the Boundary Waters. In addition to wearing it on your head, hang your headlamp from the tent ceiling to light up the tent, or use it to make shadow puppets on the tent wall.

Island

We paddle to a large island on the northeast end of the lake and set up camp.
I place the gas stove on the rocks surrounding the fire grate and fry freshly
caught fish. A hungry and brave mouse darts out from a crack between the
rocks and snatches a fallen crumb of breading just inches from me. I shout
in surprise. Then I watch with amazement as this brazen mouse darts out
again and again to steal crumbs for its supper. I can tell that this mouse is an
experienced thief!

Islands are pieces of land surrounded on all sides by water. Islands are
just like the other parts of this wilderness area. They have the same
wildlife and plants on them. Look for islands in most lakes in
the Boundary Waters.

J

Jack Pine

Gathering firewood I find a jack pine tree that has toppled over. I cut off as many branches as I can carry and drag them back to camp. Once the campfire is burning I line up a row of jack pine pinecones on the edge of the fire grate, where they will get hot, and I wait for them to open. The sap holding the pinecone closed melts when exposed to the fire, causing the pinecone to open and its seeds to fall out. The jack pine needs fire in order to spread its seeds.

Try getting jack pine pinecones to open when you have a campfire. Have an adult help you to put the pinecones near the fire and retrieve them once they have opened. Plant some seeds near your camp.

Kindling

When I leave the tent in search of kindling, raindrops are still dripping off the tree branches. Kindling are the tiny twigs and pieces of bark that can be used to start a fire. I look for kindling in places protected from the rain: under low-hanging tree branches and beneath the overturned canoe. I bring handfuls of kindling to the fire grate, put pieces of birch bark in a pile and make a pyramid with the sticks around the birch bark. This fire should start with only one match.

Kindling needs to be dry to start a fire easily. When you first reach a campsite you may wish to collect dry kindling and wood and store it in a place that will remain dry if it rains. You can also make fire starters at home. See the back of this book for the Boy Scout method of making fire starters.

Loon

The pair of loons are beautiful in their formal black-and-white outfits. They glide effortlessly ahead of our canoe. Suddenly they dive under the water and disappear. I scan the surface of the lake in every direction as the seconds tick away. Finally, off to the left, one loon pops to the surface, followed shortly by the second one. I smile and giggle in surprise.

The common loon is the Minnesota state bird and is a familiar sight in the Boundary Waters. The loon's call is beautiful and lonesome as it echoes across the lake. A fun game to play is to guess where a loon will resurface after it dives underwater.

28

Moose

Keeping my eyes on the unsuspecting moose we paddle our canoe silently at a snail's pace. Nearby the moose plunges its head underwater and chomps vegetation growing on the bottom of the lake. The water splashes and drips as it lifts its head from the lake. We watch the moose dine for minutes before it spies us, turns slowly toward shore and ambles off into the woods.

Moose are the largest kind of deer. They are equally comfortable on land and in the water. The males have large antlers that fall off each winter. Moose are only one of the many kinds of animals you can observe in the Boundary Waters. There is a list of animals in the back of this book; check off those you see while camping.

Northern Pike

We catch three northern pike before supper and leave the largest one in the lake tied to a fallen log. We'll eat this fish for breakfast. In the morning I walk to the water's edge to retrieve the fish, and all that is left on the stringer is the fish's head! During the night an animal—an otter, a snapping turtle or maybe another northern pike—ate the rest of the fish and stole our breakfast.

Northern pike are long, lean fish with razor-sharp teeth! But fry a northern pike in oil and it tastes delicious!

Ojibwe

The Ojibwe man in the back of the boat uses a long pole to push the canoe through the thick wild rice plants. An Ojibwe woman bends the tops of the wild rice plants over the canoe and hits them with sticks. The wild rice grains fall into the canoe. When the canoe is full the man and woman return to shore with their harvest.

The Ojibwe were just one of the many groups of native peoples who lived and traveled in the Boundary Waters before non-native settlers moved to this region. Wild rice was an important food for them and helped them to survive during the long, cold Minnesota winters. Imagine what it would be like to harvest wild rice using a canoe!

Pictographs

The waves lap gently against the black rock cliff as I sit in the canoe and search the rock face for the tell-tale red color of ancient pictographs. There! I've found them! I gaze in awe at the pictures of red-colored moose, stick people and canoes.

These pictographs may have been drawn up to 500 years ago! Look for pictographs on rock ledges and cliffs along lake edges. See the back of this book for a list of references to help you find pictographs in the Boundary Waters.

Quiet

I wake up as the sun is just beginning to climb over the eastern horizon. I leave the warmth of my sleeping bag and sit on a rock with a view of the calm lake. The only sound is the lonesome call of a loon across the lake. As the echo of the loon's cry fades away, I hear a white-throated sparrow sing its distinct song, "Old Sam Peabody, Peabody, Peabody." Then all is quiet again. The quiet moments such as these are what make spending time in the Boundary Waters so special.

Find a time in the Boundary Waters when you can sit quietly and listen to the sounds around you. What do you hear?

Rapids

We hear them before we see them. We are canoeing down a river in the Boundary Waters and the thunderous sound is coming from rapids up ahead. We land at the portage well before the rapids. During the portage we stop along the trail and look at the river flowing swift and high below. We see standing waves, holes, boils and whirlpools in this rough stretch of rapids. It is awe-inspiring and frightening at the same time.

Rapids are rough and fast sections of water on a river. Always be cautious when you come upon rapids. It is safest to portage your canoe and gear around them using a portage trail.

S'mores

I move the two marshmallows skewered on a stick a little closer to the bright red coals of the campfire. Just a little more roasting and they will be perfectly brown. Suddenly, the marshmallows burst into flames! I blow out the flames and examine the damage. Some black ashes cling to the marshmallows, but they are still edible. I place a piece of chocolate candy bar on a graham cracker, slide the two marshmallows on and put another graham cracker on the top. I take a bite and taste the crunchy, sticky and sweet treat. Delicious! Of course, I want another one.

A camping trip just isn't complete without s'mores. All you need are marshmallows, graham crackers and chocolate bars. See if you can improve on this recipe. What could you substitute for these ingredients?

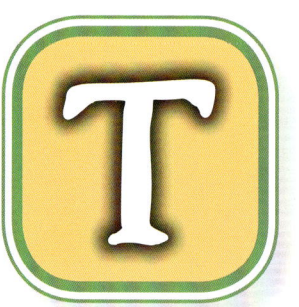

Tent

Three sharp, long whistles echo across the lake. I am in a canoe near the far shore when the whistle pierces the air. There is an emergency back at camp! I race back to camp and spy a fellow camper standing on the shoreline. He points to the water and shouts, "The wind blew the tent into the lake!" We haul the wet tent back onto shore, string clotheslines between trees and hang up the tent to dry. Luckily our tent is dry by bedtime.

Tents are lightweight shelters used for camping. They can be big or small and are easily moved to a new campsite. Draw a picture of your idea of a neat tent. What would it look like? What features would it have?

Underwater

The spring air is crisp and cold as we paddle toward the portage at the end of the lake. In the distance we see white objects sticking out of the water. We paddle over to investigate and find a moose carcass. Above the water the bones are white and clean. Under the water, hair and tissue cling to the bones and move slowly with the motion of the waves. In winter, animals had picked the bones above the ice clean, but they couldn't get the rest of the moose under the frozen lake.

There are many opportunities to observe the natural life cycle of plants and animals in the Boundary Waters. Look for animals and plants at different life cycle stages as you travel and camp.

Voyageurs

The men sing a lively French tune as they paddle the 25-foot canoe that carries their tools, cloth and trinkets. The song helps them to paddle together and pass the time. They wear colorful shirts, moccasins and red sashes. When they portage they carry several 90-pound packs over miles of rough and rocky trails. Voyageurs were colorful and hardworking men who used canoes to transport goods and animal pelts.

Make up your own song about traveling in the wilderness, and sing it with the others in your group. See the back of the book for an example of a song you could sing.

W

Whitecaps

The surface of the lake looks like a blue cake with waves of white-tipped frosting. The huge waves wash over the bow of the canoe and splash my lap and feet. It feels like I am riding a rodeo bull as the canoe climbs to the crest of a wave, hesitates and falls into the space between waves. We aim for the side of an island that is protected from the wind and dig our paddles deep into the water. I breathe a huge sigh of relief as the canoe finally glides into the protected area behind the island.

Whitecaps are waves that have a white top on them. This usually happens when a strong wind creates large waves. When whitecaps appear it is safest to wait for calmer waters before venturing out on the lake.

X-ing (crossing)

We canoe down the little creek as it winds through the valley. Up ahead the creek widens into a pond, and we spy a beaver dam blocking the way. We maneuver the canoe parallel to the mud and branches, lift the vessel over the dam and climb back into it. We will repeat this process many times on our way.

Beavers make dams, ponds and lodges as protection from predators. Also, a beaver dam serves as a clue that a beaver crosses the creek there. X-ing is another way of representing a crossing. A fun Boundary Waters activity is to look for clues that tell you where animals might cross your path. Then create a sign that identifies the crossing. Perhaps you will make a moose X-ing sign where you find moose poop. The sillier the idea, the more fun you can have playing this game.

Yoke

I bend down and grasp the yoke of the canoe with one hand and the side of the canoe with the other. With one smooth motion I swing the canoe up over my head and rest the yoke pads upon my shoulders. I trudge carefully up the rocky portage trail. I admire wildflowers growing along the way. Over the hill and back down into a low area, I cross a small stream and hop cautiously from rock to rock, before marching back up another incline. My eyes scan the woods ahead of me in search of blue lake and sky that signal the end of this portage.

A yoke is a sturdy piece of wood in the middle of the canoe that is used to support the canoe when it is portaged. The canoe remains parallel to the ground while it rests on a person's shoulders. Portaging a canoe is a little like balancing a book on your head. Practice balancing a book on your head, and when you have the hang of it, make an obstacle course to try while balancing the book.

Zipper

The food bag is hanging high above the ground. The fire is out, and the canoe is pulled onto shore and tied to a tree. Above me the stars are shining brightly. I look around camp one last time and then unzip the tent. Zzzzzzzzzip goes the zipper as I pull the tent zipper open, step in and then pull it closed. I snuggle into my sleeping bag and listen to the sounds of the night: a loon, waves lapping on the shore, the wind through the pines and the slap of a beaver's tail. They lull me to sleep. Goodnight Boundary Waters....

Zzzzzzzzzzzzzzzzzzzzzzzzzzzzzzzzzzzzzzzzzzzzzzzzzzzzzzzzzzzzz

You can purchase CDs that have the sounds of the Boundary Waters recorded on them. Or you could bring a recorder and make your own soundtrack. Some people listen to these sounds to help them fall asleep. Other people listen to them when they wish to be reminded of the Boundary Waters.

Birds You Might See in the BWCAW

Directions: Place a check mark beside each bird that you see while on a trip in the Boundary Waters Canoe Area Wilderness.

Goose

Heron

Owl

Loon

Jay

Raven

Grouse

Grosbeak

Sparrow

Chickadee

Gull

Duck

Eagle

Finch

Animals You Might See in the BWCAW

Directions: Place a check mark beside each animal that you see while on a trip in the Boundary Waters Canoe Area Wilderness.

- Deer
- Muskrat
- Beaver
- Lynx
- Turtle
- Otter
- Wolf
- Mouse
- Squirrel
- Moose
- Bear

Blueberry Pancake Recipe

Mix together the following dry ingredients:

1½ Cups of flour

3 Tablespoons of sugar

2 Teaspoons of baking powder

½ Teaspoon of salt

Mix in the following liquid ingredients:

2 eggs

1½ Cups of milk (you can use powdered milk and water)

2¼ Tablespoons of cooking oil

½ Teaspoon of vanilla

Mix all ingredients for a minute or two. Put oil in the bottom of your skillet and warm the skillet over medium heat. Pour the pancake batter into the skillet and add 5–10 blueberries immediately to each pancake. Flip once and remove when both sides are golden brown. Serves 3–4 people.

NOTE: MAKE SURE TO HAVE AN ADULT HELP YOU WITH THIS RECIPE.

Campsite Rating Sheet

Directions: First write down the location of the campsite. For example: The southeast island campsite on Isabella Lake. Then provide a rating for each of the campsite's features. You can write comments or notes in the comments section. There is also an "other" section, so you can create your own campsite features.

LOCATION: _____

Beach area to land canoe, fish, swim _____

Fire grate, available wood and cooking/campfire area _____

Tent pad _____

Trees for hanging food _____

Other _____

4 = Perfect!   3 = Better than most   2 = Just OK   1 = Not so good   (or use your own rating scale)

Voyageur Song (sung to the tune of "Row, Row, Row Your Boat")

Paddle, paddle, paddle your canoe in the Boundary Waters

Hear the loons, see the eagles, try to catch a fish

Paddle, paddle, paddle your canoe in the Boundary Waters

Find a campsite on the shore and cook a yummy dish

Pattern for a Miniature Duluth Pack

Materials:

8"x11" piece of construction paper

Two pieces of construction paper ¾" wide by 4" long

Transparent tape

9" piece of yarn

Button (½ to ¾" diameter)

Begin with an 8"x11" piece of construction paper. Complete the steps outlined below:

Step 1: Fold the 8"x11" piece of paper on the dotted lines.

Steps 2A/2B: Cut on the dotted line and fold the side flaps forward on the dotted line, then fold the middle flap forward on the dotted line.

Steps 3A/3B: Fold each side back and tape to the back of the paper.

Step 4: Take one ¾"x4" piece of paper, and tape the ends of it to the back of the paper as shown at right. Do the same with the other strip of paper. These will be the straps, like the straps on a real Duluth pack.

Step 5: Cut a 6" inch piece of yarn and double it over. Put a hole in the middle of the front flap, 1 inch from the bottom of the flap. Thread the yarn through the hole from the inside of the flap, and tie a knot on each end of the yarn. The yarn will make a loop that sticks out of the front of the flap.

Step 6: Cut a 3" inch piece of yarn, and thread the button onto the yarn. Thread the yarn through the inside lower flap, 1 inch from the bottom and in the middle of the flap. Knot the yarn so that the button is on the outside of the flap and is just below the upper flap. Place the yarn from the top front flap over the button on the bottom front flap to secure the pack. Now you have a miniature Duluth pack!

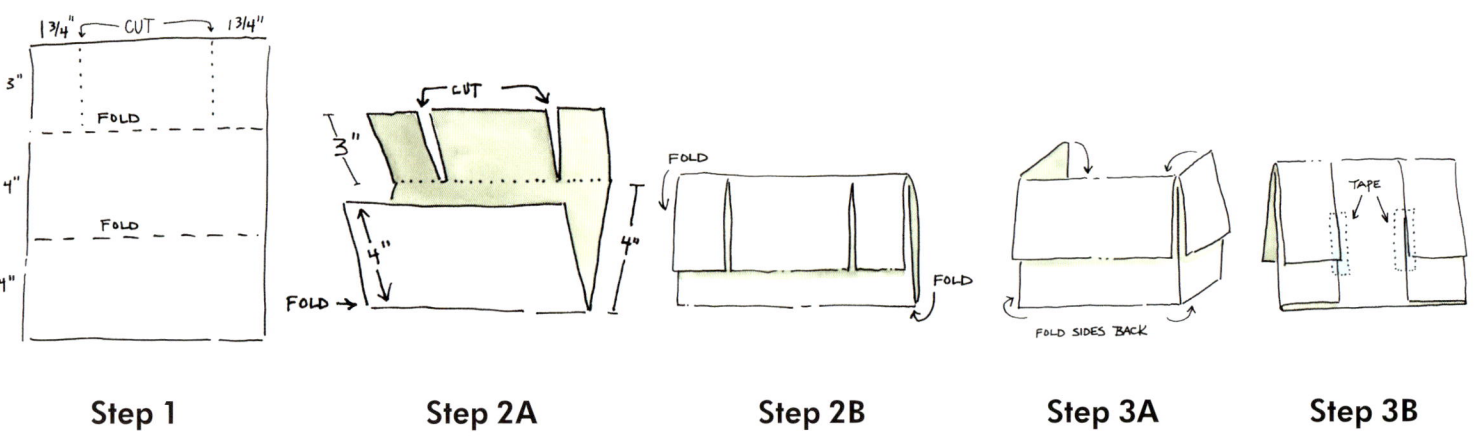

Step 1   **Step 2A**   **Step 2B**   **Step 3A**   **Step 3B**

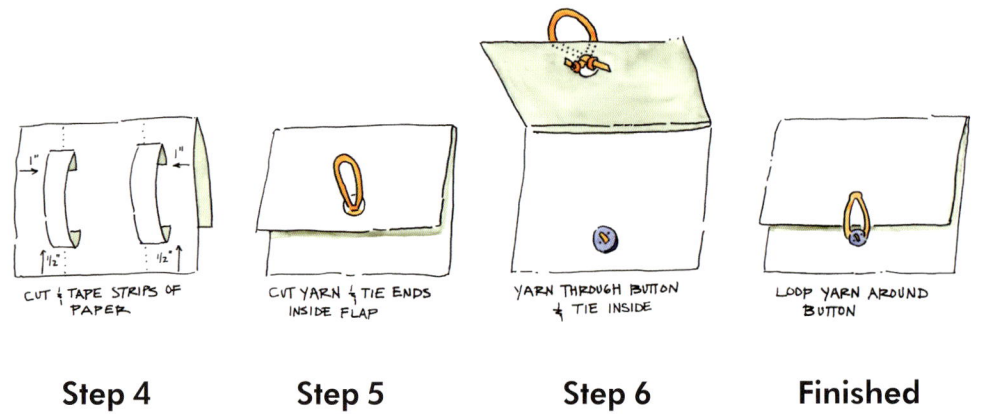

CUT & TAPE STRIPS OF
PAPER

CUT YARN & TIE ENDS
INSIDE FLAP

YARN THROUGH BUTTON
& TIE INSIDE

LOOP YARN AROUND
BUTTON

Step 4   **Step 5**   **Step 6**   **Finished**

The Boy Scout Method of Making Fire Starters

Materials:

1 empty paper egg carton

Approximately one pound of wax candles

A few cups of sawdust

A few cups of lint

Step 1: Separate the top of the egg carton from the bottom of the egg carton.

Step 2: Put sawdust into each section of the egg carton.

Step 3: Melt wax until it is liquid.

Step 4: Pour melted wax over the sawdust.

Step 5: Push some lint into the wax and cover with more sawdust before the wax cools.

Step 6: After it cools, cut out each compartment of the egg carton. Each one is a fire starter.

When you want to make a fire, place one of the pieces of the fire starter in the middle of the pyramid of kindling, then light the firestarter.

CAUTION: AN ADULT SHOULD MELT THE WAX AND HELP YOU POUR IT. THE WAX NEEDS TO BE MELTED SLOWLY AND AT A LOW TEMPERATURE.

Recommended Reading

GENERAL KNOWLEDGE

Beymer, Robert, and Dzierzak, Louis. *Boundary Waters Canoe Area: Eastern Region*. Berkeley, CA: Wilderness Press, 2009.
Beymer, Robert, and Dzierzak, Louis. *Boundary Waters Canoe Area: Western Region*. Berkeley, CA: Wilderness Press, 2009.
Jacobson, Cliff. *Boundary Waters Canoe Camping*. Guilford, CT: Falcon Guides, 2012.

HISTORY

Heinselman, Miron. *The Boundary Waters Wilderness Ecosystem*. Minneapolis, MN: University of Minnesota, 1996.

TRIP PLANNING

Apps, Jerry. *Campfires and Loon Calls: Travels in the Boundary Waters*. Golden, CO: Fulcrum, 2011.
Beymer, Robert, and Dzierzak, Louis. *Boundary Waters Canoe Area: Eastern Region*. Berkeley, CA: Wilderness Press, 2009.
Beymer, Robert, and Dzierzak, Louis. *Boundary Waters Canoe Area: Western Region*. Berkeley, CA: Wilderness Press, 2009.
The Boundary Waters Journal. Ely, MN: Michelle and Stuart Osthoff (publishers).
Churchill, James. *Paddling the Boundary Waters and Voyageurs National Park*. Guilford, CT: The Globe Pequot Press, 2003.
Jordahl, Van, and Strom, Gerald. *20 Great BWCA Trips: Exploring the Boundary Waters Canoe Area*. Cambridge, MN: Adventure Publications, 2011.

CAMPING WITH CHILDREN

Carlson, Laurie, and Dammel, Judith. *Kids Camp!: Activities for the Backyard or Wilderness*. Chicago, IL: Chicago Review Press, 1995.
Olsson, Helen. *The Down and Dirty Guide to Camping with Kids: How to Plan Memorable Family Adventures and Connect Kids to Nature*. Boston, MA: Roost Books, 2012.

FISHING

Furtman, Michael. *A Boundary Waters Fishing Guide*. Minocqua, WI: NorthWord, 1990.

PLANTS AND ANIMALS

Stensaas, Mark. *Canoe Country Flora: Plants and Trees of the North Woods and Boundary Waters*. Duluth, MN: Pfeifer-Hamilton, 1996.
Stensaas, Mark. *Canoe Country Wildlife: A Field Guide to the North Woods and Boundary Waters*. Duluth, MN: Pfeifer-Hamilton, 1993.

PICTOGRAPHS

Furtman, Michael. *Magic on the Rocks: Canoe Country Pictographs*. Duluth, MN: Birch Portage Press, 2002.

WEBSITES

Website to make Boundary Waters reservations: www.recreation.gov
Directory of Outfitters, Resorts and Lodging near the Boundary Waters: www.bwca.cc
Boundary Waters Trip Planning Guide: www.fs.usda.gov/Internet/FSE_DOCUMENTS/stelprdb5259796.pdf